William Shakespeare

Romeo and Juliet

Retold by Helen Street
Illustrated by Charly Cheung

REAL READS

Ernst Klett Sprachen
Stuttgart

First published in 2010 by Real Reads Ltd
Stroud, Gloucestershire, UK
www.realreads.co.uk

1. Auflage 1 6 5 4 3 | 2020 19 18 17 16

Alle Drucke dieser Auflage können nebeneinander benutzt werden, sie sind untereinander unverändert. Die letzte Zahl bezeichnet das Jahr des Druckes.

Inhaltlich identisch zur Ausgabe mit Schutzumschlag.

Internetadresse: www.klett-sprachen.de

Umschlaggestaltung: Sandra Vrabec
Annotationen und Übungen: Cornelia Scherer

Designed by Lucy Guenot
Typeset by Bookcraft Ltd, Stroud, Gloucestershire

Printed by: AZ Druck- und Datentechnik

ISBN 978-3-12-576194-0

9 783125 761940

CONTENTS

THE CHARACTERS

The Capulets and the Montagues

These two families have been at war with each other since anyone can remember. What will it take for them to end their feud?

Juliet

The only daughter of the Capulets, Juliet is about to fall in love for the first time. What desperate measures must she take to stay true to her love?

Juliet's Nurse

Her nurse has cared for Juliet since she was a baby. Nurse loves Juliet, but will she always be on her side?

Tybalt

Capulet's fiery nephew. His challenge to Romeo will end in bloodshed, but whose blood will it be?

Romeo Montague

When Romeo meets the love of his life, everything changes for this romantic youth. But will his happiness be short-lived?

Benvolio and Mercutio

Romeo's friends. Gentle Benvolio doesn't like trouble, unlike the fearless Mercutio who goes looking for it.

Friar Laurence

Friar Laurence wants to make peace between the feuding families. But where will his plans lead the two young lovers?

ROMEO AND JULIET

Chorus

Two households, both alike in dignity,
In fair Verona, where we lay our scene,
From ancient grudge create new rivalry
That leads two star-crossed lovers to their deaths.
See now, two servants from opposing sides
Begin a brawl that will ignite this tale.

ACT ONE, SCENE ONE
A STREET IN VERONA

A Capulet servant bites his thumb as a Montague servant goes by.

Montague servant

Do you bite your thumb at me?

Capulet servant

I do bite my thumb, sir.

Montague servant

But do you bite your thumb at *me*, sir?

Capulet servant

And if I do, sir?

Montague servant

Then you insult me, sir.

Capulet servant

And so?

Montague servant

Then draw your sword!

Capulet servant

Gladly! You dog of Montague!

Benvolio enters.

Benvolio

Put up your swords! You know not what you do!

Tybalt enters.

Tybalt

What? Fighting with servants, Benvolio?
Coward, you'll find a better foe in me!

They fight. Capulet and Montague, the heads of their respective families, arrive on the scene.

Capulet

Fetch me a sword.
My enemies are drawn against me.

Montague

You villain, Capulet!

There is a general fight. The Prince enters.

Prince

Enough! Throw down your weapons.
Hold, I say!
If ever you disturb our streets again,
Your Prince condemns you to be put to death.
Away! And leave the city streets in peace.
You, Capulet, shall go along with me,
And Montague, come you this afternoon
To hear what else I have to say.

Everyone leaves except Montague and Benvolio.

Montague

Who stirred up our old quarrel once again?

Benvolio

I came upon your servant fighting with
The servant of your enemy, my lord.
I drew my sword to part them but alas,
The fiery Tybalt with his own sword drawn
Came on the scene to urge them on.
I had to fight to save myself from him.
Came more and more to fight on either side
Until the Prince arrived and parted us.

Montague

O where is Romeo? Saw you him today?
Right glad I am he was not at this fray.
His mood is always sad and secretive.
If only I could know why this was so.

Benvolio

Here comes your son, perhaps he'll talk to me.
If you depart, I'll speak to Romeo.

Montague leaves.

Good morrow, cousin. Why look you so sad?

Romeo

I am in love with she who loves me not.

Benvolio

Then give her up and seek out other maids.
At Capulet's, tonight, there is a ball,
The beauties of Verona will be there.

Romeo

None fairer than my Rosaline, I swear.

Benvolio

That may be so but let us merry be
And dance and feast and pass the night away.

Romeo

Not I, my heavy heart will weigh me down.

Mercutio enters.

Mercutio

Nay, gentle Romeo, we must have you dance!
Put on your masks, let's not delay, the night
Draws on, and gentlemen, we must away.

Romeo, Benvolio and Mercutio leave.

ACT ONE, SCENE TWO
CAPULET'S HOUSE

Chorus

Look now within the house of Capulet
The lady wishes conference with her child.

Lady Capulet enters.

Lady Capulet

Nurse, where's my daughter? Call her forth to me.

Nurse enters.

Nurse

Juliet! Your mother calls. Juliet!

Juliet enters.

Juliet

Madam, I am here. What is your will?

Lady Capulet

To talk of marriage now you are fourteen.

Nurse

Thou wast the prettiest babe that e'er I nursed:
If I might live to see thee married once,
I have my wish.

Lady Capulet

The brave Count Paris seeks you for his love.

Nurse

A handsome man, young lady, such a man!

Lady Capulet

This night you shall behold him at our feast.
Look well on him and tell me what you think.

Servant

Madam, the guests are come.

Lady Capulet

We follow thee. Come, Juliet.

Nurse

Go, girl, seek happy nights to happy days.

ACT ONE, SCENE THREE
CAPULET'S HALL

Chorus

Now come the merry guests in party masks
To Capulet's grand hall to dance and feast,
And in disguise, a certain Romeo
Shall soon discover his true destiny.

Capulet

Welcome, gentlemen! Ladies that have their toes
Unplagued by corns shall have a dance with you!
More light, you knaves, and turn the tables up
And quench the fire, the room is grown too hot.
Come musicians, play a lively measure!

Romeo

What lady's that, who glides about the room
Like a rich jewel that sparkles in my sight?
Did my heart love till now? I will say nay
For I ne'er saw true beauty till this night.

Tybalt

I know his voice. He is a Montague.
Now, by the stock and honour of my kin,
To strike him dead I hold it not a sin.

Capulet

Young Romeo, is it?

Tybalt

'Tis he, that villain Romeo.

Capulet

Hold back, young cousin, let him well alone.
The people hereabouts speak well of him.
I would not for the wealth of all this town
Here in my house do him a grievous harm.

Tybalt *(aside)*

I will be patient till we meet again.

Romeo *(to Juliet)*

Forgive the roughness of my hand on yours.
My lips are here to smooth it with a kiss.

Juliet

Noble sir, there is nothing to forgive.

Nurse

Madam, your mother craves a word with you.

Juliet leaves.

Romeo

Who is her mother?

Nurse

Well, young sir,
Her mother is the lady of this house.

Romeo

She is a Capulet? It cannot be!
Alas, I have fallen for my enemy.

Benvolio

Let's leave this place, the dance is past its best.

Romeo

Yes, that is so – far more than you could know.

Romeo's group leaves.

Juliet

Good nurse, who is yonder gentleman?

Nurse

His name is Romeo, and a Montague;
The only son of your great enemy.

Juliet *(aside)*

How could I have known? But now too late,
My heart is given to one that I should hate.

Nurse

Come, let's away. The strangers have all gone.

ACT TWO, SCENE ONE
THE GARDEN OF THE CAPULETS

Chorus

In Romeo's heart a new love grows, for now
Is fair Juliet the centre of his world.
But as a Montague, he may not knock
Like suitors do upon the entrance door.
And so, by stealth, he climbs the stony wall
That guards the garden of the Capulets.

Romeo

But, soft! What light through yonder window breaks?
It is the east, and Juliet is the sun!
See how she leans her cheek upon her hand!
O, that I were a glove upon that hand,
That I might touch that cheek!

Juliet

Ay, me!

Romeo

She speaks.

Juliet

O Romeo, Romeo! Why must you be Romeo!
Deny your father or else change your name,

And if you love me, I'll no longer be
A Capulet. Yet 'tis but a name.
What's in a name? That which we call a rose
By any other name would smell as sweet.

Romeo

Call me but love, and I'll be new baptised;
Henceforth I never will be Romeo.

Juliet

My ears have yet not drunk a hundred words
Of thy tongue's uttering, yet I know the sound:
Art thou not Romeo, and a Montague?

Romeo

Neither, fair maid, if either thee dislike.

Juliet

How came you here, good Romeo, and why?
The orchard walls are high and hard to climb
And the place death, considering who thou art
If any of my kinsmen find thee here.

Romeo

With love's light wings did I o'erfly these walls
For stone defences cannot keep love out.

Juliet

If they do see thee, they will murder thee.

Romeo

I have the night to hide me from their eyes,
But let them find me. Here I'd rather die
Than live forever waiting for your love.

Juliet

I should be shy and blush with flaming cheeks
For you have overheard my private thoughts,
But gentle Romeo, let us not pretend.
Dost thou love me? I know thou wilt say 'ay'.

Romeo

Lady, by yonder blessed moon I swear ...

Nurse *(calling from within the room)*

Madam!

Juliet

I must go! If thy love is honourable
And if thy purpose marriage, send me word
Tomorrow of when and where we meet.

Nurse

Madam!

Juliet *(to nurse)*

I will be there.

(to Romeo)

Good night, good night!
Parting is such sweet sorrow
That I shall say goodnight till it be morrow.

ACT TWO, SCENE TWO
OUTSIDE THE CHURCH

Chorus

In dawn's fresh light goes Romeo to the church,
To seek out Friar Laurence for his help.

Friar

The grey-eyed morn smiles on the frowning night,
Chequering the eastern clouds with streaks of light;
And flecked darkness like a drunkard reels
From forth day's path and Titan's fiery wheels.
Now, ere the sun advance his burning eye,
The day to cheer and night's dank dew to dry,
These herbs and flowers must I gather up
For cures and potions for the healing cup.

Romeo enters.

Romeo

Good morrow, father!

Friar

Benedicite!
Such earliness – I think I hit it right,
Our Romeo hath not been in bed this night.

Romeo

O father, know my heart's dear love is set
On the fair daughter of rich Capulet;
We met, we woo'd, and made exchange of vow.
I pray you, father, marry us right now.

Friar

Holy Saint Francis! What a change is here!
First Rosaline, now Juliet thy dear.
The tears for your first love are barely dry.
But come, young Romeo, come, go with me;
The wedding rites I will perform for thee,
For this alliance may so happy prove,
To turn your households' rancour to pure love.

ACT THREE, SCENE ONE
A STREET IN VERONA

Chorus

Come to Verona's streets where good friends meet,
And pass the time away in idle talk.

Benvolio and Mercutio enter.

Mercutio

Where the devil should this Romeo be?
Came he not home last night?

Benvolio

Not to his father's, his servant said.

Mercutio

The cause must surely be this Rosaline.

Benvolio

Tybalt, the kinsman of old Capulet,
Hath sent a letter to his father's house.

Mercutio

A challenge, on my life.

Benvolio

Romeo will answer him.

Mercutio

Alas, poor Romeo, he is already dead!
Stabbed through the heart with cupid's arrow.
He has gone soft with love!

Benvolio

But here he is!

Romeo enters.

Mercutio

My friend, you gave us all the slip last night.

Romeo

Forgive me, good Mercutio, I had
Important things to do.

Mercutio

Yes, I am sure!

Juliet's nurse enters.

Nurse

Good morrow gentlemen. Can any of you tell me
Where I might find the young Romeo?

Romeo

I am he.

Nurse

A word in private, sir, I beg of you.

Mercutio

Watch out, my friend, she may invite you home!
But we'll away and meet you at your house.

Benvolio and Mercutio leave.

Nurse

My gentle lady bid me search you out.
But sir, if you should double deal with her,
And she so young, it will go ill with you.

Romeo

Fear not, good nurse, and tell your sweet mistress
To find excuse to go to church today,
And there, this afternoon, shall she be wed.

Nurse

Now god in heaven bless you! She'll be there.

Nurse and Romeo leave separately.

ACT THREE, SCENE TWO
A STREET IN VERONA

Chorus

In secret then do Romeo and Juliet
Make holy vows of marriage in the church.
Their feuding parents must not know the truth,
And so they part: she, to her father's house,
And Romeo to find his friends somewhere
Out on Verona's hot and dusty streets.

Benvolio

Good friend Mercutio, let's not stay here.
The day is hot, the Capulets about,
And, if we meet, we shall not 'scape a brawl.

Mercutio

A brawl *you*'re more likely to begin!

Benvolio

I do protest! Tis you who quarrels more.
But look, here come the Capulets. Beware.

Tybalt and his men arrive.

Tybalt

Gentlemen, a word with one of you.

Mercutio

Only a word? Let's make it something more.

Tybalt

Give me some excuse and you shall have it!

Mercutio

Why wait? My sword and I are ready.

Romeo enters.

Tybalt

Romeo, you are naught but a villain.
And I have come for satisfaction.

Romeo

I will not fight with you, good Capulet.

Mercutio

And let him walk away? That shall not be.
Tybalt, be quick and draw your sword
Or else this fight will be unfair to thee!

Romeo

Gentlemen!
Put down your swords, I beg of you.

Tybalt and Mercutio fight.

Romeo

Tybalt! Mercutio! The Prince himself
Forbids this brawling in Verona's streets.
Hold, Tybalt! Hold, Mercutio!

Romeo intervenes, but Mercutio is stabbed by Tybalt.

Mercutio

A plague on both your houses, I am hit.

Benvolio

What, art thou hurt?

Mercutio

Why the devil came you between us?

Romeo

I thought all for the best.
Courage, man, the hurt cannot be much.

Mercutio

Help me into some house, Benvolio,
Or I shall faint. A plague on both your houses!

Benvolio helps him off.

Romeo

My own dear friend has got this mortal wound
On my behalf. My love for Juliet
Has made me gentle and perhaps too soft.

Benvolio returns.

Benvolio

O Romeo, Romeo, brave Mercutio's dead!

Romeo

Tybalt, I will not walk away this time.
Mercutio's soul hovers above us now.
He waits for thee to keep him company!

Romeo and Tybalt fight. Tybalt dies.

ACT THREE, SCENE THREE
CAPULET'S HOUSE

Chorus

Meantime, inside the house of Capulet,
Juliet waits, impatient and alone.

Juliet

O hurry, sun, and speed across the sky
That night may come and bring me Romeo!
And let the darkness hide my blushing cheeks
Till I have learned the ways of married love.
Give me my Romeo; and, when he shall die,
Take him and cut him out in little stars,
And he will make the face of heaven so fine
That all the world will be in love with night.
So tedious is this waiting, it is like
The day before a party to a child
Who has new clothes but may not wear them yet.

Nurse enters.

Nurse

O dreadful news! Thy cousin Tybalt's dead.
And 'twas Romeo's hand that shed his blood.

Juliet

Romeo! Thou wicked angel! How could
You have deceived me so. I thought you good,
But you had murder in your very heart.

Nurse

There is no trust or honesty in men.

Juliet

What have I said? He is my husband
And must have had good cause to do the deed.
My cousin was the villain in the fight.
My husband lives that Tybalt would have slain.
But what of Romeo? Where is he now?

Nurse

He is banished, and must leave tonight.

Juliet

O woe, then I shall never be a wife.

Nurse

I know where he is hiding, and will go
And bring him to you for a last farewell.

ACT THREE, SCENE FOUR
THE CHURCH

Chorus

Though Romeo flees the scene of Tybalt's death,
He can't escape the judgement of the Prince.
Within the friar's church he hides and weeps,
Lamenting his misfortune and his loss.

Romeo

Friar, you say my fate is banishment?
Alas, that word is worse than 'death' to me.

Friar

Be thankful, Romeo, for such mercy.

Romeo

'Tis torture, and not mercy: heaven is here,
Where Juliet lives; and every cat and dog
And little mouse, every unworthy thing,
Live here in heaven and may look on her;
But Romeo may not.

Friar

Ungrateful man! Have you not eyes to see?
A pack of blessings lights upon thy back!
Juliet, who loves you, lives, and so do you,
Who Tybalt would have killed, and now the Prince
Has ordered exile instead of cruel death.

Nurse arrives.

Nurse

O sir, my mistress weeps and calls for thee.

Friar

Go to her, Romeo, and comfort her.
And do not stay past dawn but get you gone
To Mantua where you must stay until
I have devised a plan to bring you home.

ACT THREE, SCENE FIVE
CAPULET'S GARDEN

Chorus

One night to be a husband and a wife,
One night alone before the last goodbye,
For, if the Prince's men should capture him,
Young Romeo this day will surely die.

Juliet

Wilt thou be gone? The dawn is still far off.
It was the nightingale, and not the lark
That sang in yonder pomegranate tree.
Believe me, love, it was the nightingale.

Romeo

It was the lark, the herald of the morn.
Night's candles are burnt out, and joyous day
Stands tiptoe on the misty mountaintops.
I must be gone and live, or stay and die.

Juliet

Stay yet awhile. Do not be gone so soon.

Romeo

Let me be put to death! I am content
To stay if Juliet wills it. 'Tis not day.

Juliet

It is, it is! Be off, be gone, away!

It is the lark that sings so out of tune.

O, now be gone; more light and light it grows.

Romeo

More light and light;

More dark and dark our woes!

Nurse *(from the house)*

Madam!

Juliet

Nurse?

Nurse

Your lady mother is coming to your chamber.

The day has broken. Be careful, look about.

Romeo

Farewell, farewell! One kiss and I will leave.

Juliet

O think'st thou we shall ever meet again?

Romeo

We shall, my sweet, and all these woes some day
Will be but stories in our time to come.

Romeo leaves and Lady Capulet enters.

Lady Capulet

Daughter, are you up? I bring you good news.

Juliet

What is it, I beseech your ladyship?

Lady Capulet

You have a caring father, Juliet,
Who has arranged for you a joyful day,
For Thursday next shall be your wedding day.
Noble Paris has sought you for his bride.
Your father has consented, happy child.

Juliet

He shall not make me then a joyful bride.
This is too soon to wed. Pray tell my lord
And father I will not marry yet.

Lady Capulet

Here comes your father; tell him so yourself,
And see how he will take it at your hands.

Capulet enters.

Capulet

Ah, wife. Have you delivered our good news?

Lady Capulet

Aye, sir, but mark, she will have none of it.
I would the fool were married to her grave.

Capulet

She will have none of it? And thanks us not
For such a worthy match? I tell thee what,
Get thee to Saint Peter's church on Thursday
Or never after look me in the face.

Juliet

Good father, I beseech you on my knees
Hear me with patience but to speak a word.

Capulet

Speak not, reply not, do not answer me:
My fingers itch. Wife, we scarce thought us blest
That god had lent us but this only child;
But now I see this one is one too much,
And that we have a curse in having her.

Nurse

My lord, you are to blame to scold her so.

Capulet

Quiet! You hold your tongue, you mumbling fool.

Lady Capulet

Be calm, dear sir, you grow too hot and vexed.

Capulet

Be you my child, then marry who I say;
If not, then beg, starve, perish in the streets,
For by my soul I'll ne'er acknowledge thee.
Nor what is mine shall never do thee good.

Capulet leaves.

Juliet

Is there no pity sitting in the clouds
That sees into the bottom of my grief?
O! Sweet my mother, cast me not away!
Delay this marriage for a month, a week.

Lady Capulet

Talk not to me, for I'll not speak a word.
Do as thou wilt, for I have done with thee.

Lady Capulet leaves.

Juliet

Have you some words of comfort for me, nurse?

Nurse

Since Romeo is banished and dare not
Come to your defence on pain of death,
I think it best you marry with the Count.

Juliet

Speak'st thou from thy heart?

Nurse

And from my soul, too.

Juliet

Well, thou hast comforted me marvellous much!
Go in and tell my lady I am gone,
Having displeased my father, to Friar Laurence,
To make confession and to be absolved.

ACT FOUR, SCENE ONE
THE CHURCH

Chorus

Poor Juliet without her Romeo,
Forsaken by an angry family
And doomed to wed a man she does not love,
Turns now for guidance to her only friend.

Friar

Ah, Juliet, I already know thy grief.
I hear you must be married Thursday next.

Juliet

O father, tell me how I may prevent it,
Or else this knife shall put an end to me.
Be not so long to speak, I long to die
If what thou say'st cannot put things right.

Friar

Hold, daughter! I do spy a kind of hope.
If, rather than to marry the Count Paris
Thou hast the strength of will to slay thyself,
Then it is likely you will undertake
A thing like death to remedy this ill.

Juliet

O! Bid me leap, rather than marry Paris,
From off the battlements of yonder tower!

Friar

Hold, then; go home, be merry, give consent
To marry Paris: Wednesday is tomorrow.
Tomorrow night when you have gone to bed
Drink of this vial and through thy veins shall run
A cold and drowsy sleep. No pulse shall beat,
No warmth, no breath, shall testify thou livest.
Thy family will think you dead and take you
To the family tomb. Meanwhile shall Romeo
Know of my plan and come to rescue thee.

Juliet

Give me then the potion. I have no fear.

Friar

I'll send a friar with speed to Mantua
To take a letter to Romeo. Now go.

Juliet

Love give me strength. Farewell, dear father.

Chorus

Juliet returns and gives the welcome news
That she consents to wed her father's choice.
So happy is Lord Capulet that he
Brings forward by a day the marriage rites.

Juliet

I have a faint cold fear thrills through my veins
That almost freezes up the heat of life.
Tonight I must this potion drink, or else.
What if this mixture does not work at all?
Shall I be married then tomorrow morn?
What if it be a poison, which the friar
Has given me to drink to have me dead
Because he married me before to Romeo?
But no, I know he is a holy man.
I will do it. Romeo, I drink to thee.

ACT FIVE, SCENE ONE
MANTUA

Chorus

Alas, for these poor lovers fate is cruel.
The letter telling Romeo the plan
Is not received, and from another source
He hears the dreadful news: his wife is dead.

Romeo

Well, Juliet, I'll lie with thee tonight.
A deadly poison will I bring with me,
To sleep forever in your company.
Here is the wretched apothecary.
Hold, here is forty ducats, man; let me have
A dram of poison, for I'm tired of life.

Apothecary

Such fatal drugs I have, but Mantua's law
Forbids their sale on pain of death, good sir.

Romeo

But I can see you live in poverty.
The world is not your friend, nor is the law.
Then be not poor, but break it and take this.

Apothecary

I do this only of dire need.
Put this in any liquid thing you will
And drink it off; and, if you had the strength
Of twenty men, you'd die immediately.

Romeo

There is thy gold, worse poison to men's souls,
Doing more murders in this loathsome world,
Than these poor mixtures that thou mayst not sell.
Go, buy some food and put weight on your bones.
Come, cordial – not poison – go with me
To Juliet's grave; for there must I use thee.

ACT FIVE, SCENE TWO
CAPULET'S FAMILY TOMB

Chorus

In grief rides Romeo from Mantua,
To be with Juliet and say goodbye.

Romeo

Here is the tomb. Here is my love! my wife!
Death, that hath sucked the honey of thy breath,
Hath had no power yet upon thy beauty.
Your lips are crimson still. Your glowing skin
Shows not death's pale appearance on your face.
Here will I stay with thee. Eyes, look your last.
Arms, take your last embrace! And, lips, seal now
With this faithful kiss an eternal vow.
Here's to my love! *(drinks poison)*
Thus with a kiss, I die.

Romeo dies. A few moments later Friar Laurence enters.

Friar

Saint Francis be my speed! Juliet will wake
Amongst the dead, alone. I must make haste.
Romeo! So pale in death upon the ground.
How can this be? But wait, the lady stirs.

Juliet wakes up.

Juliet

Good friar, you are here – but where is my lord?

Shouting is heard offstage.

Friar

I hear some noise. Come, lady, come away!
Our plans have all gone wrong, I know not how.
Thy husband there lies dead, and we must flee.

Juliet

Go, get thee hence, for I will not away.

Friar

Here come the guards. I dare no longer stay.

The friar leaves.

Juliet

Poison, I see, hath been his timeless end.
Have you drunk all and left no friendly drop
To help me follow thee? I'll kiss thy lips.
Perhaps some poison still remains on them.
Thy lips are warm.

Shouts are heard again.

More noise! I must be quick!
O happy dagger, hide yourself in me
And let me die.

Juliet snatches Romeo's dagger, stabs herself, and dies.
The Prince enters with his attendants.

Prince
What misadventure is so early up,
That calls our person from our morning rest?

Capulet and Lady Capulet enter.

Capulet
What can it be that all do shriek so loud?

Lady Capulet
The people in the street cry 'Romeo',
And some cry 'Juliet', and then all run
In great distress towards our family tomb.

Prince
What fear is this which startles in our ears?

Attendant
Sovereign, here lies Romeo dead by poison,
And by his side is Juliet, still warm,
Though we had thought her dead two days ago.

Capulet
O, heaven! O wife, look how our daughter bleeds!

Montague enters.

Montague
What cruelty is this, that Romeo
Should go before me to his grave?

Friar Laurence is brought on by an attendant.

Friar
My liege, this sorry tale I will explain
That you may judge my actions right or wrong.
Romeo, there dead, was husband to that Juliet;
And she, there dead, that Romeo's faithful wife.
I married them, and their secret wedding day
Was Tybalt's death day. Then came banishment.
They could not live without the other one.

Prince
Where be these enemies? Capulet! Montague!
See, what a scourge is laid upon your hate,
That heaven finds means to kill your joys with love.

Capulet

O brother Montague, give me thy hand;
My daughter sweet would wish it so.

Montague

And here is mine, my son would want it too.

They shake hands.

Prince

A gloomy peace this morning with it brings.
The sun for sorrow will not show his head.
Go hence, to have more talk of these sad things,
For never was a story of more woe
Than this of Juliet and her Romeo.

Taking things further

Glossary

Abbreviations:
lit *literary*
old *old-fashioned*
sb *somebody*
sth *something*

Page 4

feud [fjuːd] a long and bitter hostility, conflict
desperate ['desprət] having lost all hope
measure *Maßnahme*
to stay true to remain loyal, committed, faithful

Page 5

fiery ['faɪəri] wild, terrible
bloodshed killing
short-lived passing quickly, temporary
friar [fraɪə] *Mönch*
feuding ['fjuːdɪŋ] being enemies

Page 7

dignity rank, status
ancient grudge long-lasting hatred
rivalry ['raɪvəlri] conflict
star-crossed unlucky
brawl [brɔːl] fight
to ignite *here:* to start
to bite one's thumb *(old)* a rude gesture to show that you dislike sb

Page 8

to insult to offend sb *(beleidigen)*
to draw to pull out
sword [sɔːd] long, sharp weapon
coward *Feigling*
foe *(old)* enemy
to fetch to bring sth to sb
villain ['vɪlən] evil or bad person

Page 9

to disturb to destroy the peace
to condemn to sentence *(verurteilen)*
to stir up to begin, to cause (trouble)
quarrel ['kwɒrəl] argument, fight
to part to separate
to urge sb on *jmdn. antreiben/anfeuern*

Page 10

fray fight
mood state of feeling or emotion
to depart to leave

Page 11

to seek out to look for, to try to find
maid *(old)* unmarried woman
to swear to promise
to feast *here:* to have a party

Page 12

to call sb forth *here:* to make sb go somewhere
thou wast *(old)* you were

Page 13

handsome ['hændsəm] good-looking (of a man)
to behold *(old)* to look at sb, to watch
are come *(old)* have come

Page 14

in disguise *verkleidet, here:* hidden behind a mask
destiny fate, fortune *(Schicksal)*
corn painful hard skin on one's toe *(Hühnerauge)*
knave a boy servant
to quench to put out
a lively measure *here:* a cheerful melody
to glide to move elegantly
stock ancestry, family
honour ['ɒnə] *Ehre*
kin *(old)* sb's relatives, family
to strike to hit hard

Page 15

hereabouts (from) around here
grievous serious, terrible
harm damage
aside not heard by other characters
patient *geduldig*
roughness *Rauheit, here: grobes Verhalten*
to smooth sth *here:* to make (things) better
to crave to wish for, to want

Page 16

to fall for sb to fall in love with sb

Page 18

suitor *(old)* boyfriend, bridegroom
by stealth [stelθ] secretive, undercover
to guard *here:* to protect
cheek part/side of the face
to deny to turn one's back on sb

Page 19

Yet 'tis but a name. It is only a name.
to baptise to christen, to name
henceforth from now on, in the future
drunk *here:* heard
uttering *here:* voice
Art thou not Romeo? *(old)* Are you Romeo?
orchard garden
to o'erfly to fly over

Page 21

to blush to go red in the face
to overhear to listen to secretly
to pretend to play-act
blessed *gesegnet*
honourable *ehrenhaft*
purpose wish, aim
sorrow sadness

Page 22

frowning ['fraʊnɪŋ] *here: missbilligend*
to chequer *here: beleben*
streaks long stripes
to reel *schwanken*
From forth . . . wheel away from the rising and burning sun
dank wet and cold
dew *Tau*
potion drink, mixture, elixir
Benedicite! Bless you!

Page 23

to woo to find each other attractive
vow promise to marry
to pray *here:* to beg
barely hardly, only just
rite procedure, ceremony
alliance connection
rancour ['ræŋkə] hatred

Page 25

idle easy
A challenge, on my life. I bet it is a challenge.

Page 26

to stab to kill with a knife
Cupid Roman god of love *(Amor)*
to give sb the slip to escape from sb

Page 27

to bid to ask
to double deal *doppeltes Spiel treiben, betrügen*
it will go ill with you it will be a very bad thing to do
to be wed *short for* to be wedded

Page 28

'scape escape
beware be careful, watch out

Page 29

naught nothing

Page 31

to faint to black out, to collapse
mortal deadly
wound [wuːnd] injury *(Verletzung)*
on my behalf *meinetwegen*
to hover to fly

Page 32

impatient *ungeduldig*
cut him out in *here:* turn him into
tedious ['tiːdiəs] boring
dreadful extremely unpleasant or shocking
to shed sb's blood to take sb's life

Page 33

wicked cruel, bad
to deceive to fool, to betray
deed *(lit)* Tat
to slay *(lit)* to kill
to banish sb to send sb away *(verbannen)*
woe *(lit)* unhappiness, sadness
farewell goodbye

Page 34

judgement decision, ruling, verdict
to weep to cry
to lament to complain about sth
fate destiny, God's will
mercy mildness, forgiveness

Page 35

torture *Folter*
ungrateful not thankful
blessing *here:* luck, good fortune
exile banishment
cruel *grausam*
dawn daybreak, sunrise
to devise to work out, to plan

Page 36

to capture to catch, to arrest
nightingale ['naɪtɪŋgeɪl] *Nachtigall*
lark *Lerche*
pomegranate *Granatapfel*
herald *here:* sign, indication

Page 37

to sing out of tune *falsch singen*
chamber room
look about watch out

Page 38

I beseech you I beg you, *here:* please tell me
has sought has chosen
bride woman on her wedding day
to consent to agree

Page 39

to mark *(old)* to pay attention
will have none of it won't have anything to do with it
would *here:* to wish
fool stupid person
a worthy match a good marriage
patience ['peɪʃənts] calmness
to itch *jucken*
we scarce thought us blest *wir glaubten uns nicht genug gesegnet*
lent us but this only child only gave us one child
curse *Fluch*

Page 40

to blame to say that sb is responsible for sth
to scold to tell sb off
mumbling fool *in etwa: schnatternde Ente*
vexed troubled, annoyed

Page 41

be you if you are
to starve to die of hunger
to acknowledge to accept
grief sorrow, misery
to cast away *here:* to throw out
to dare to be brave enough to

Page 42

to make confession *beichten*
to be absolved to be forgiven

Page 43

forsaken *(lit)* to be left alone by sb
doomed condemned *(verdammt)*
guidance help
to prevent to stop
be not so long don't wait too long
I long I want
to spy (sb/sth) to see
to undertake (to agree) to do sth
to remedy to cure, to heal

Page 44

to leap to jump
battlement the tower walls
vial ['vaɪəl] small bottle
veins tubes in the body
drowsy ['draʊzi] sleepy, weary
to testify to prove, to indicate
tomb grave
to rescue to save sb, to free sb

Page 46

to bring forward *vorverlegen*
faint unclear, slight
to thrill to run, to spread

Page 47

source *Quelle*
wretched *here:* poor, unhappy
apothecary *(old)* person who prepares medicines
ducat *Dukate, alte Geldeinheit*
dram a mouthful
fatal causing death

Page 48

dire [daɪə] extreme
liquid fluid
immediately [ɪ'miːdiətli] at once
loathsome hateful, horrible
cordial medicine

Page 49

to suck to take away
crimson of a dark red colour
pale white-faced
appearance *here:* expression
embrace act of taking sb in the arms
to seal confirm, guarantee
faithful loyal, devoted
eternal endless, never-ending
to make haste to act quickly
to stir to move

Page 50

go hence *(old)* leave at once *(hinweg mit dir/euch)*
guard sb who watches and protects sth
timeless *(old)* untimely, too soon
to remain to be left over

Page 51

dagger a knife-like weapon
attendant servant
misadventure misfortune, mishap
to shriek to scream, to shout
distress mental/emotional pain
to startle to disturb, to scare
sovereign ruler or monarch

Page 52

to bleed to lose blood
cruelty sth that causes pain or suffering
liege *Lehnsherr*
to judge to make up one's mind about sth
scourge *here:* punishment, great evil

Page 54

gloomy dark, cloudy

Exercises

I. Comprehension questions

Act one

Answer the questions.

1. Where is the first scene set?
2. What are the names of the two opposing families?
3. What does the Prince do to stop the fighting?
4. Who is Rosaline?
5. Why does Lady Capulet want to talk to her daughter Juliet?
6. How old is Juliet?
7. What does the Nurse think of Paris?

Act two

Answer the questions.

1. Why doesn't Romeo use the main entrance door to visit Juliet?
2. How does he get into the garden?
3. What does Romeo compare Juliet to?
4. What would happen if a member of the Capulet family found Romeo in the garden?
5. Why does Juliet have to end their secret date?
6. Why does Juliet want to meet Romeo again?
7. When and why does Romeo visit the Friar?

Act three, Scene one

Finish the sentence.

1. The first scene of the third act is set …
2. Mercutio would like to know …
3. Mercutio thinks that Romeo still …
4. Tybalt's letter to Romeo is …
5. The Nurse is looking for Romeo to …
6. The Nurse is afraid that …
7. Romeo wants Juliet to …

Act three, Scene two

Are these statements right or wrong? Correct wrong sentences.

1. Romeo and Juliet meet in the church.
2. Their parents are guests at their wedding.
3. After the ceremony they have a big party.
4. Tybalt challenges Mercutio.
5. Romeo doesn't want Tybalt and Mercutio to fight.
6. Romeo stops their brawl.
7. Benvolio is injured by the Prince.
8. Romeo feels guilty for his friend's death.
9. Romeo challenges Tybalt.
10. Tybalt kills Romeo.

Act three, Scene three

Connect the sentences by writing the correct number in the corresponding box.

1. Juliet is waiting for Romeo because	3.	for having killed her cousin.
2. The Nurse tells Juliet that	6.	to meet Romeo for a last farewell.
3. At first, Juliet condemns Romeo	2.	Tybalt is dead.
4. Later, she understands that	5.	Romeo must leave Verona.
5. Juliet finds out that	1.	she wants to show him her feelings.
6. The Nurse helps Juliet	4.	it was self-defence.

Act three, Scene four

Who says what? ***the Nurse, Romeo, the Friar***

Banishment is worse than death. Romeo

You should be thankful. Friar

Where Juliet is, there is heaven. Romeo

You are lucky that you will survive. Friar

Juliet is so sad and wants to talk to you. Nurse

You must leave tonight. Friar

Stay in Mantua till you hear from me. Friar

Act three, Scene five

Answer the questions.

1. How does Juliet try to convince Romeo that he can stay a bit longer?
2. What would happen to Romeo if the Prince's men found him?
3. Does Romeo believe that they will meet again?
4. What is Juliet's reaction to her parents' arrangement?
5. How do the parents react to Juliet's answer?
6. What will Lord Capulet do if his daughter doesn't agree to marry Paris?

What exactly is the Friar's suggestion to Juliet? Put the sentences into the correct order. Write the numbers one to nine into the boxes.

	Juliet drinks the potion.
	The family brings Juliet to the family tomb.
	Romeo comes to the tomb and rescues Juliet.
	The friar gives Juliet a potion in a small bottle.
	Juliet's family thinks she is dead.
	Romeo returns to Verona.
	The Friar sends a message to Romeo in Mantua.
	Juliet goes home and tells her parents that she agrees to marry Paris.
	Juliet falls asleep.

Explain these passages in your own words.

Juliet: My husband lives that Tybalt would have slain.
But what of Romeo? Where is he now?

Chorus: Within the Friar's church, he (Romeo) hides and weeps,
Lamenting his misfortune and his loss.

Juliet: It was the nightingale, and not the lark
That sang in yonder pomegranate tree.

Why - why - why?

1. Why does Romeo think his wife is dead?
2. Why does Romeo meet the apothecary?
3. Why does the apothecary sell the poison to Romeo although it is against the law?
4. Why does Romeo leave Mantua?
5. Why does the Friar want to flee?
6. Why does Juliet kiss Romeo's lips?
7. Why does Juliet use a dagger?
8. Why do Capulet and Montague shake hands?

II. Who is on whose side?

Make a list of characters in the play. Now sort them into three groups. Which are friends and family of Romeo? Which are friends and family of Juliet? Which are neutral?

Romeo

Juliet

neutral

III. Word search

1. Collect words and phrases from the play that express love and happiness.

2. Collect words and phrases from the play that express death and sadness.

IV. Creative writing

1. Write a love letter to Romeo or to Juliet.
   Consider the situation of the two families and bear in mind that Romeo and Juliet have just met for the first time.

2. Write Tybalt's letter to Romeo.

3. Imagine Romeo writes a letter to Juliet in which he explains how her cousin Tybalt died. Write this letter.

4. Imagine you are Juliet: What are her feelings before drinking the potion? Write a diary entry.

5. Continue the story. Imagine the next day in Verona.
   The Montague and Capulet servants meet in the streets.
   What do you think will happen? Write a new scene.